I0711246

COLORING MANDALAS BOOK´S MODEL.

BY JONATHAN THEN

CUTTING THE LINE ON THIS PAGE TO GUIDE YOU ON THE COLORING PAPER.

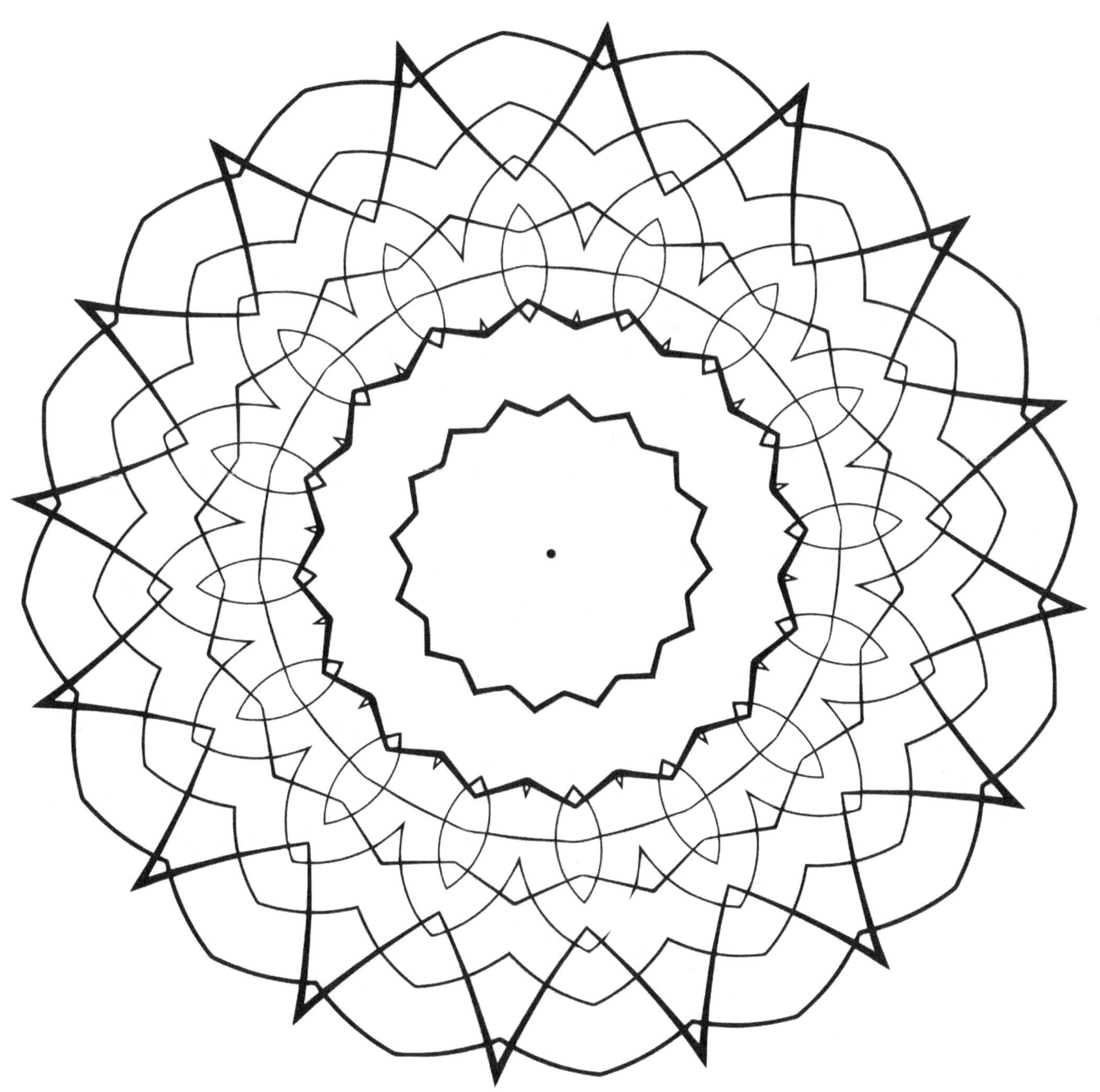

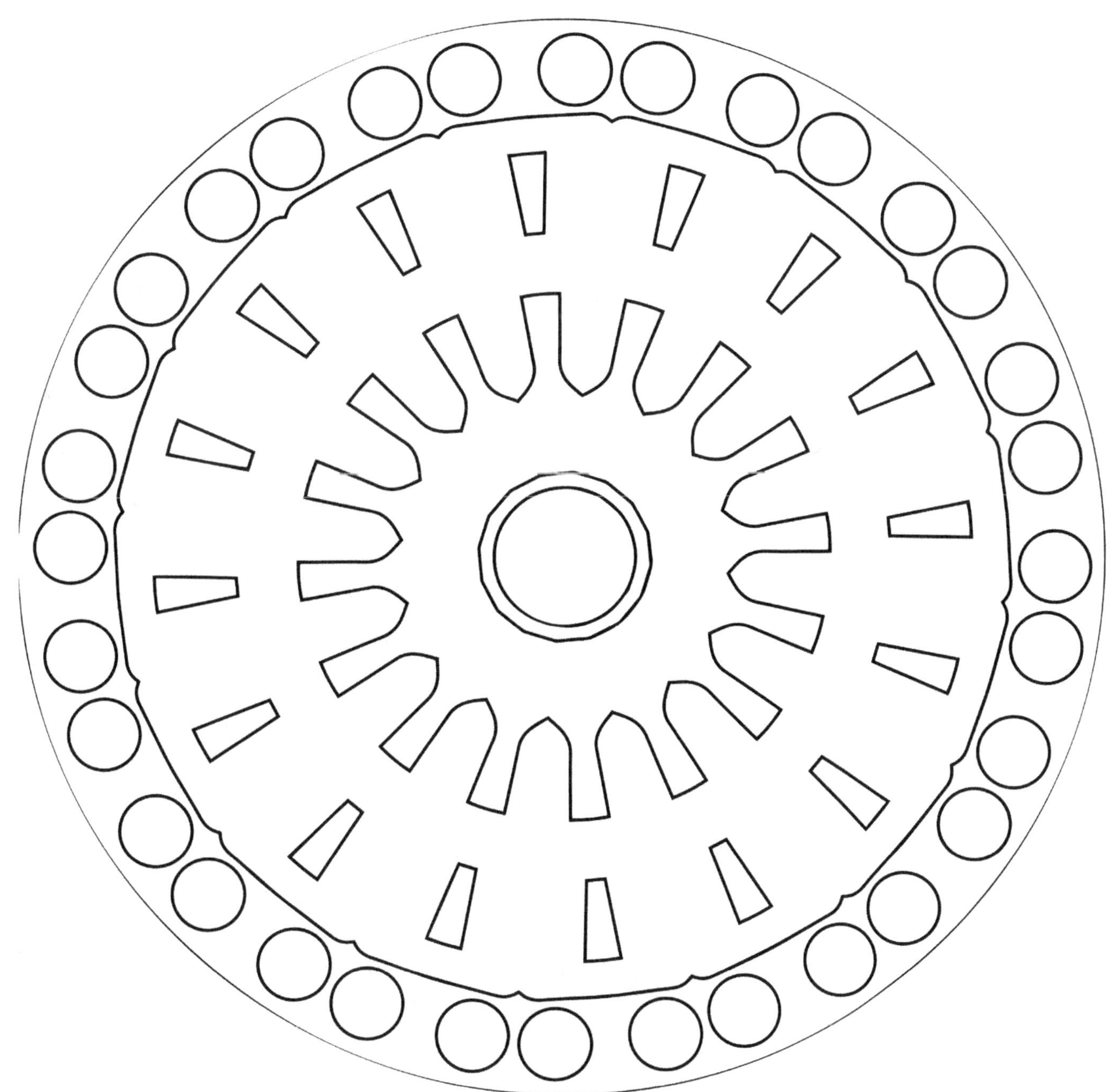

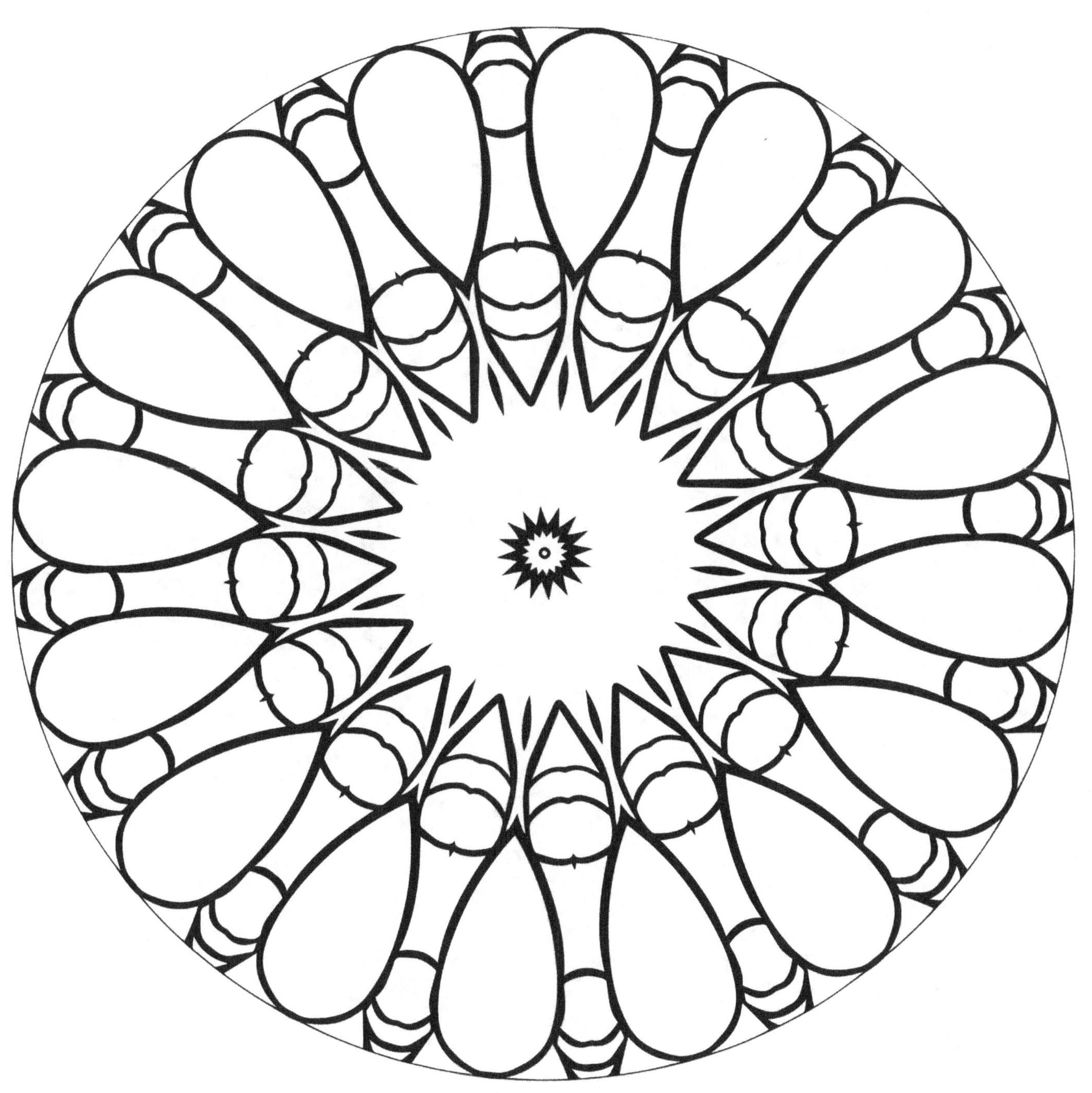

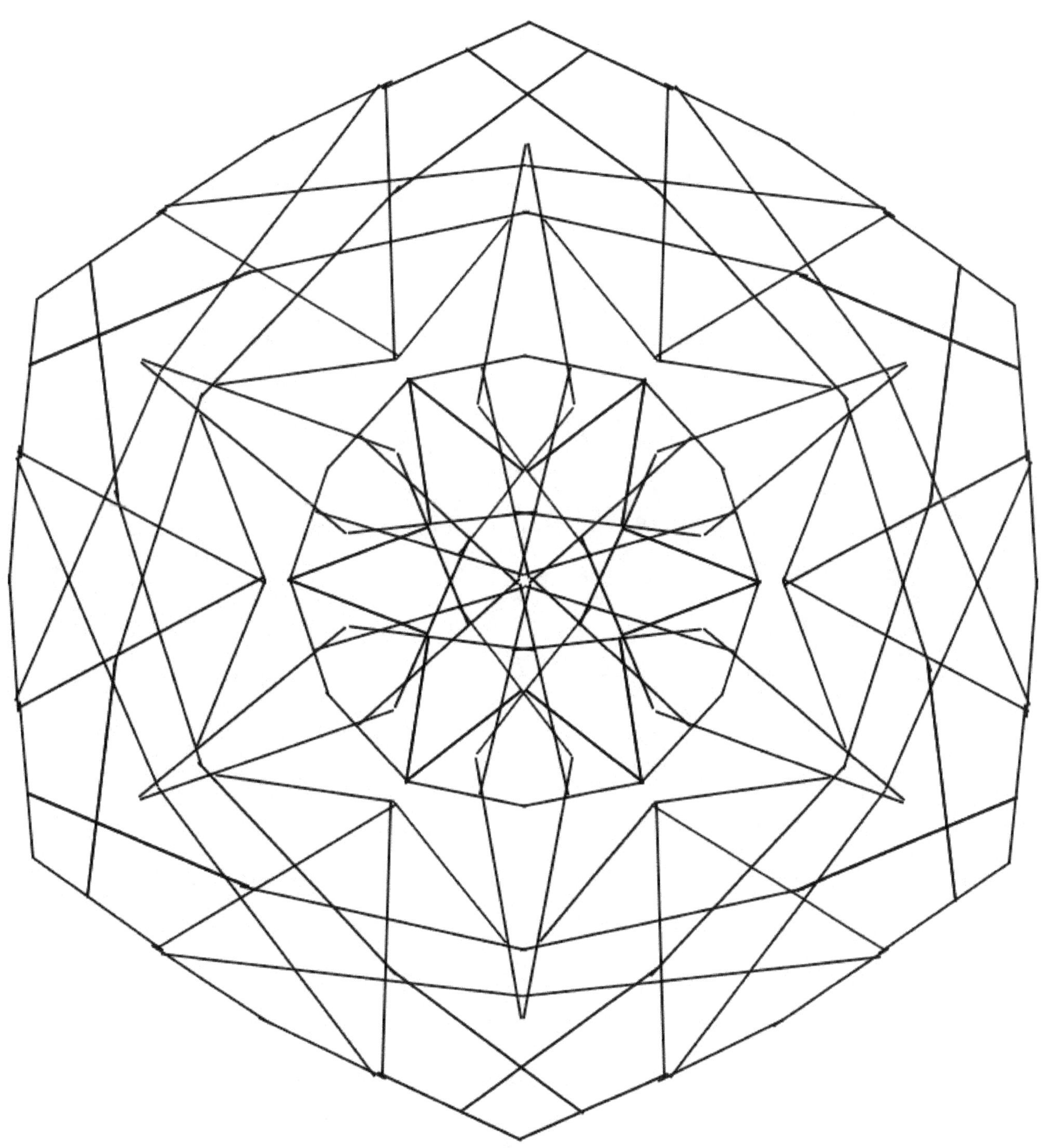

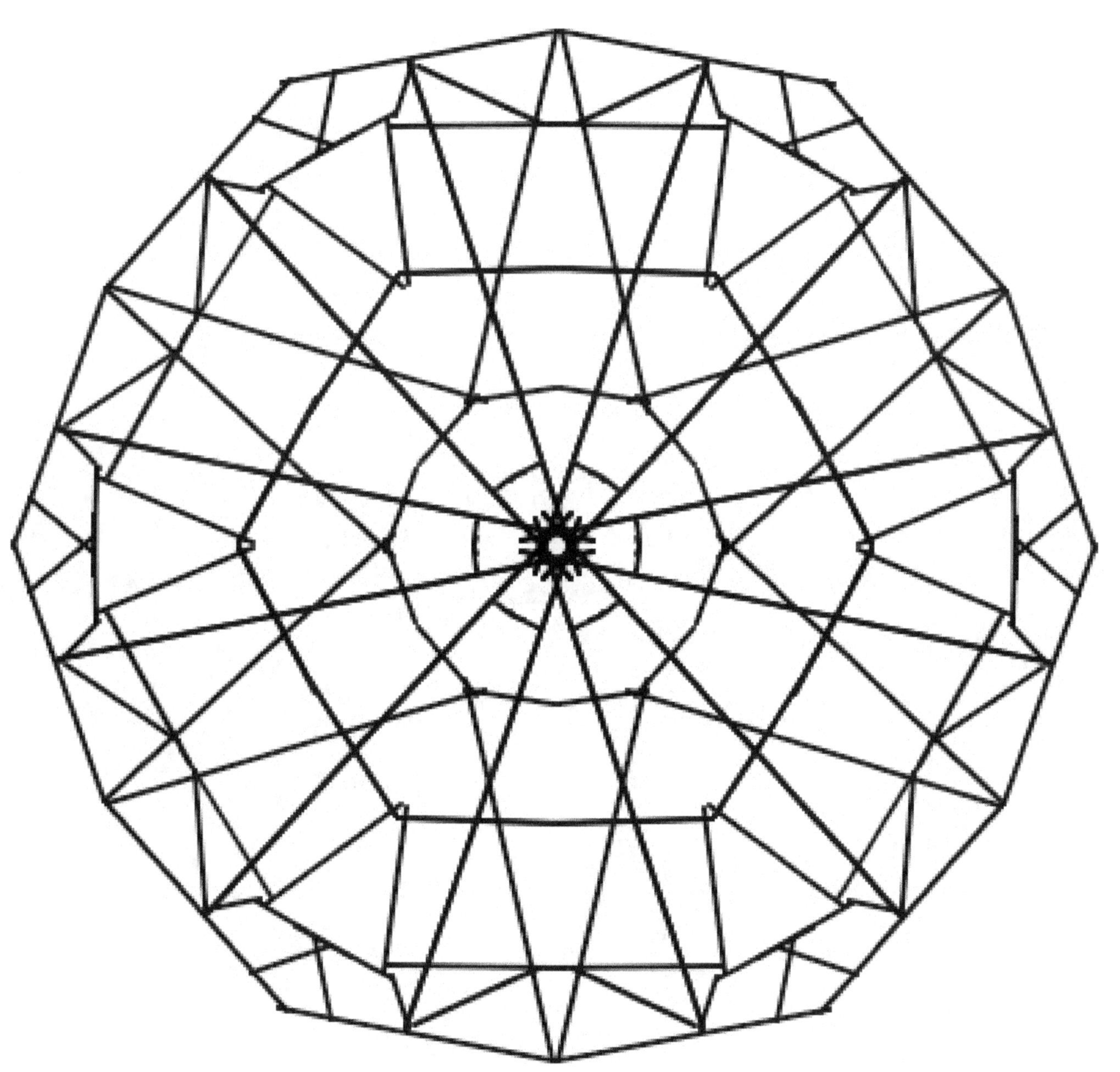

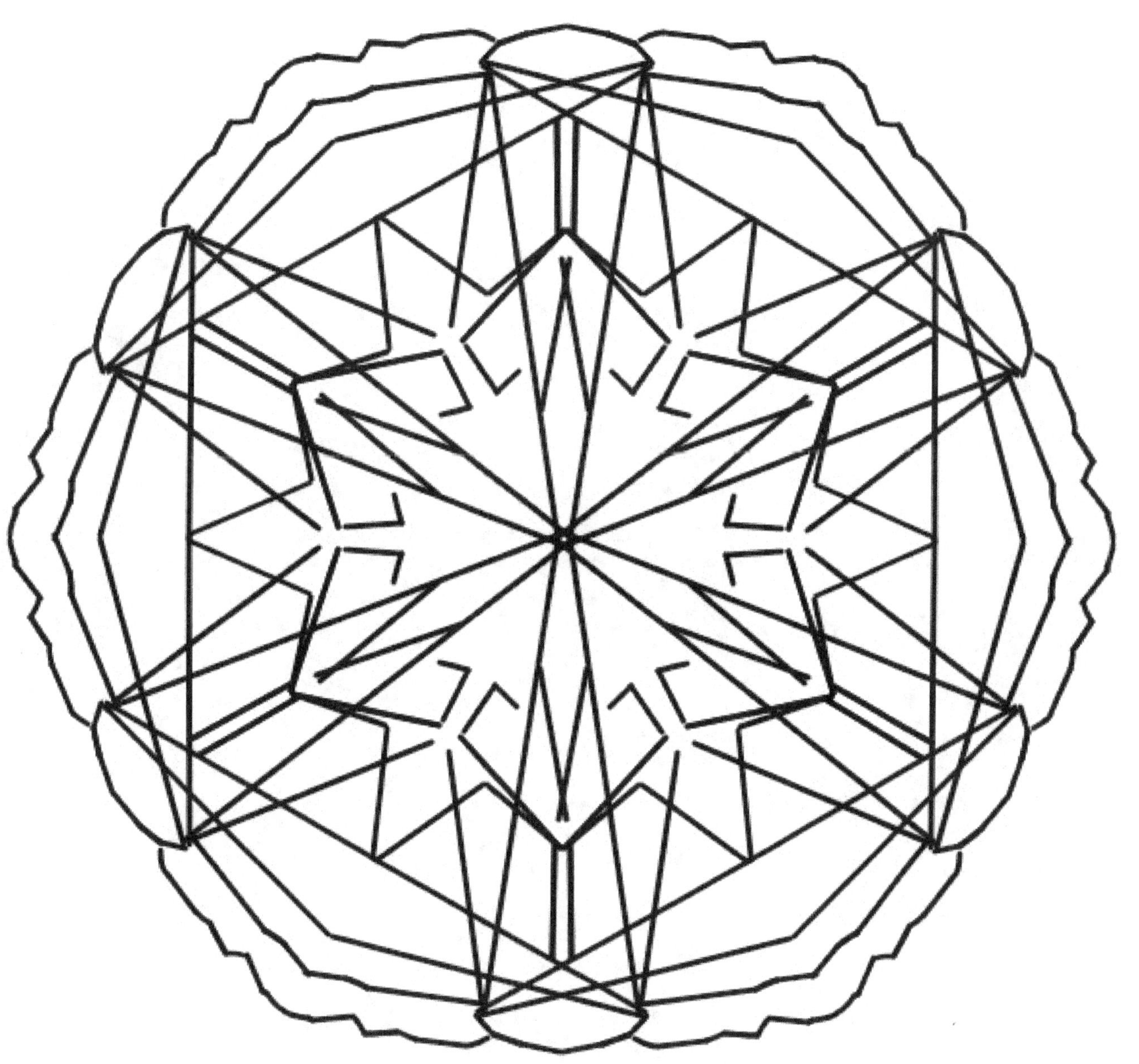

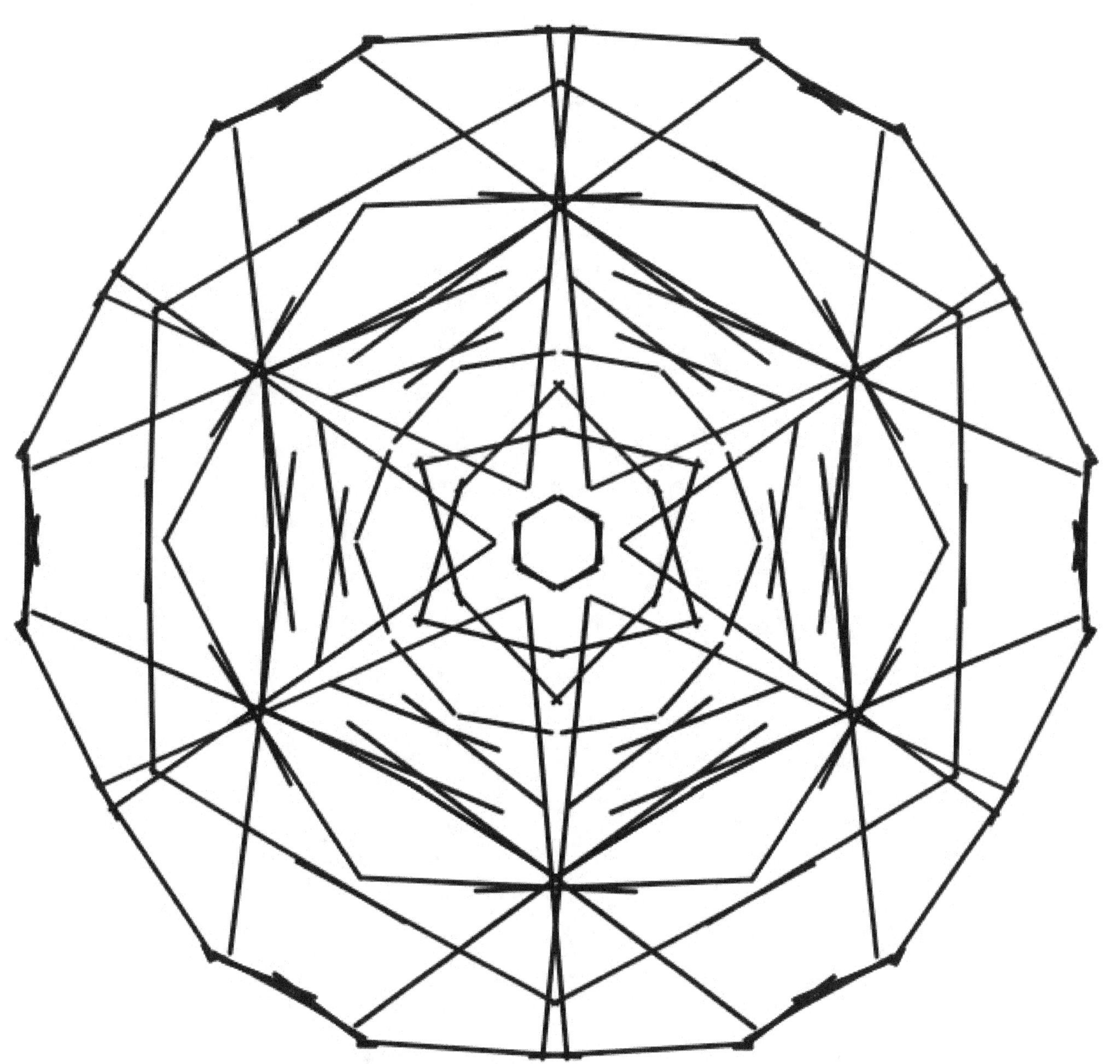

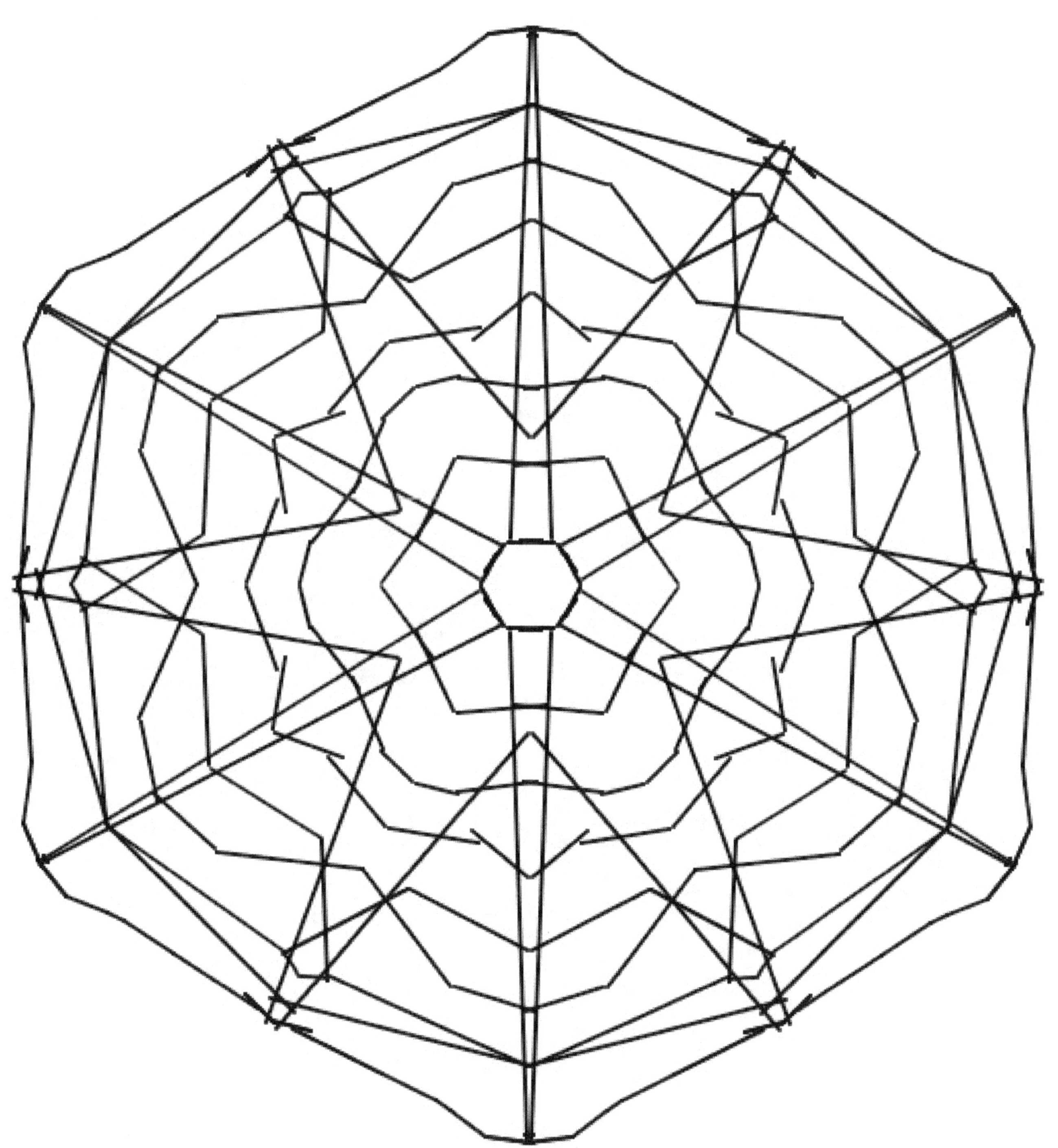

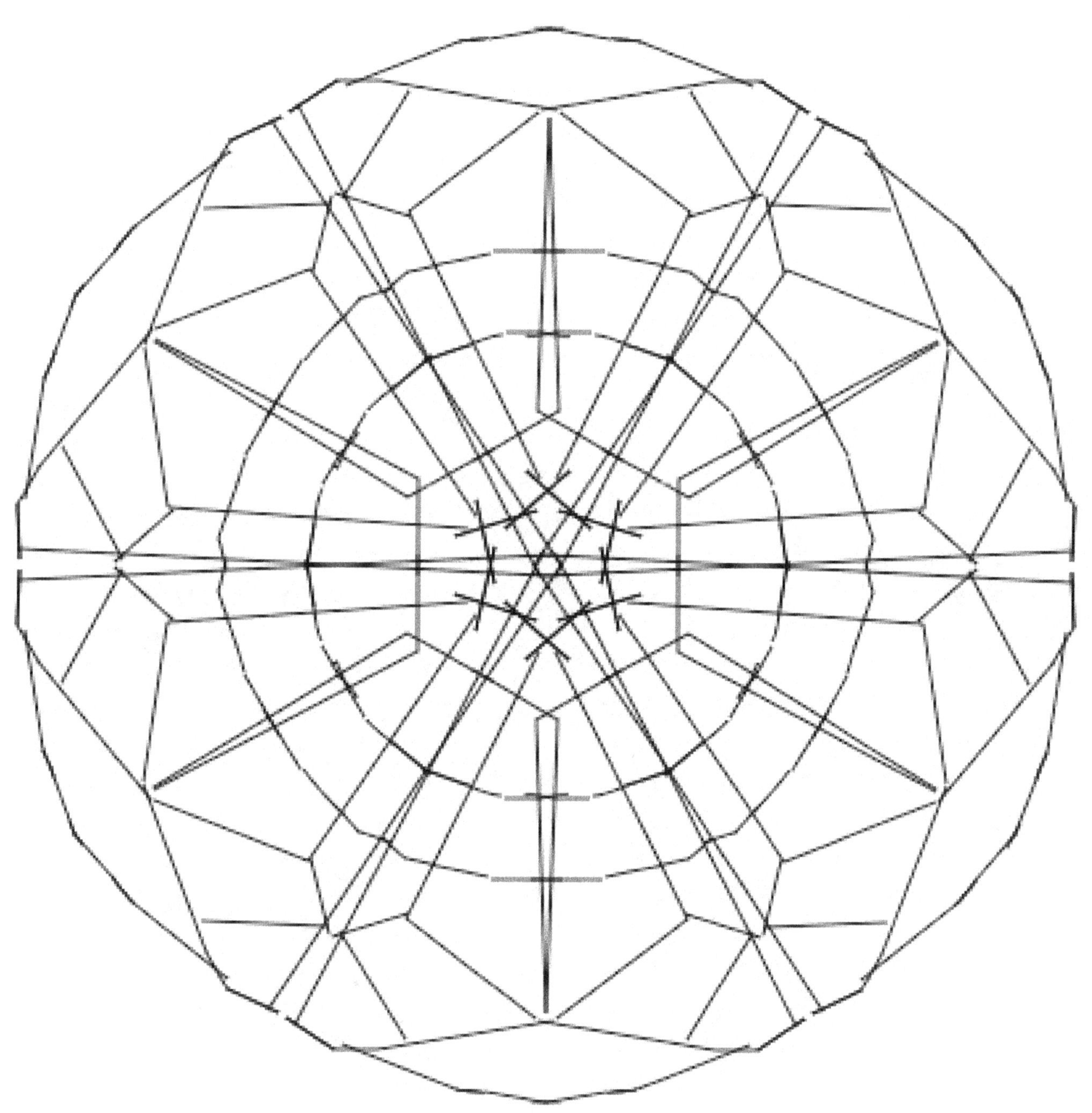

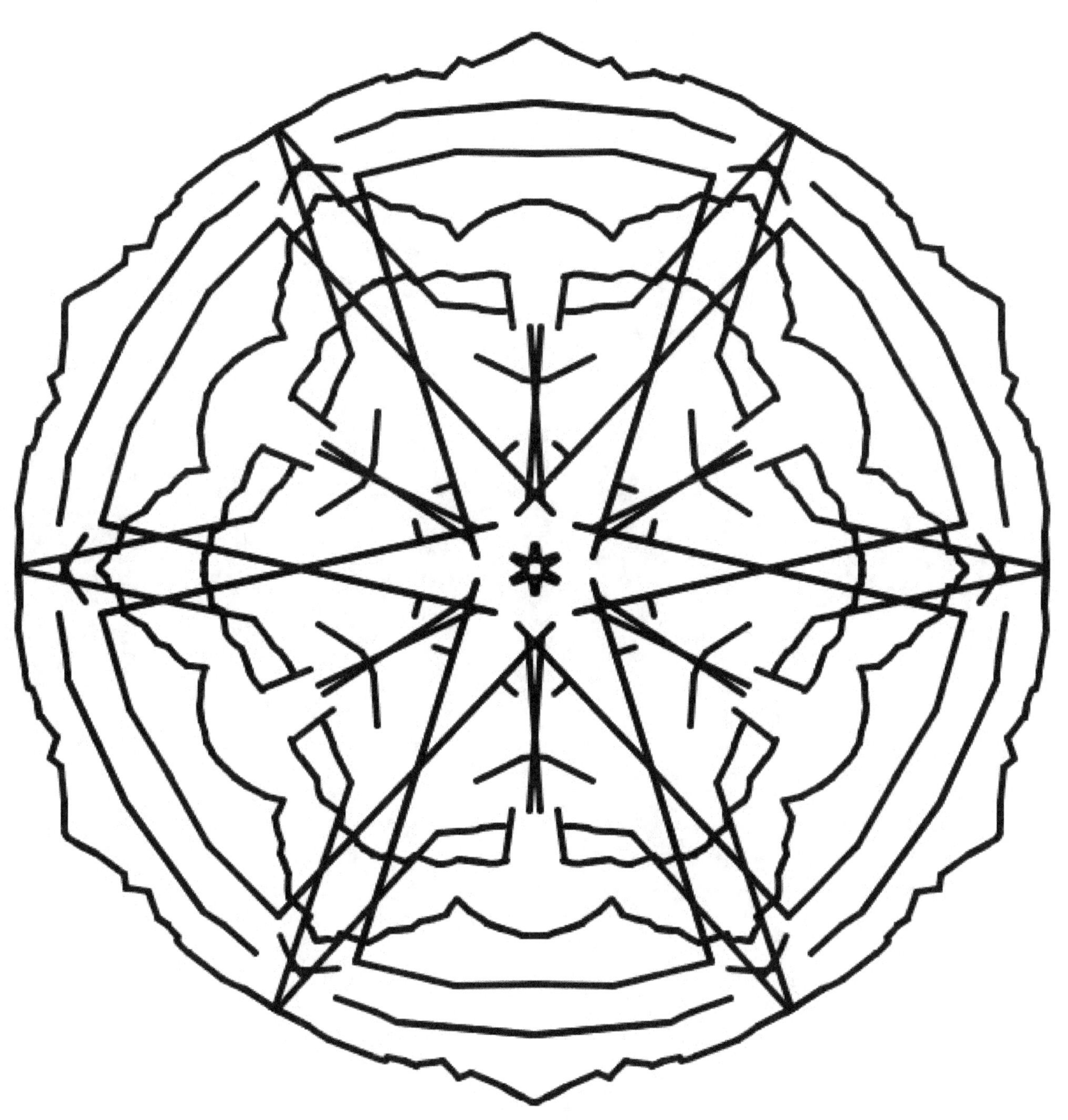

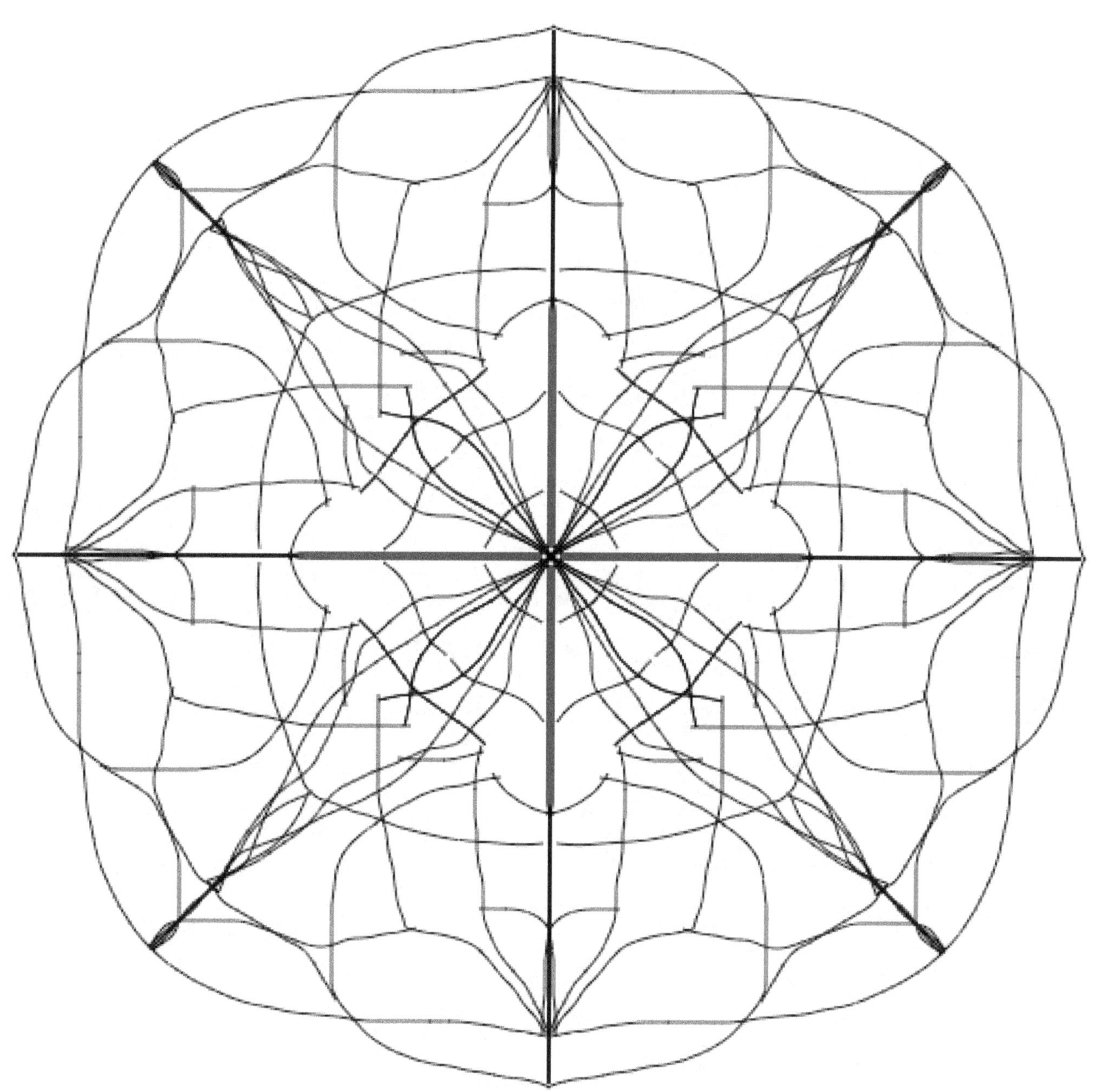

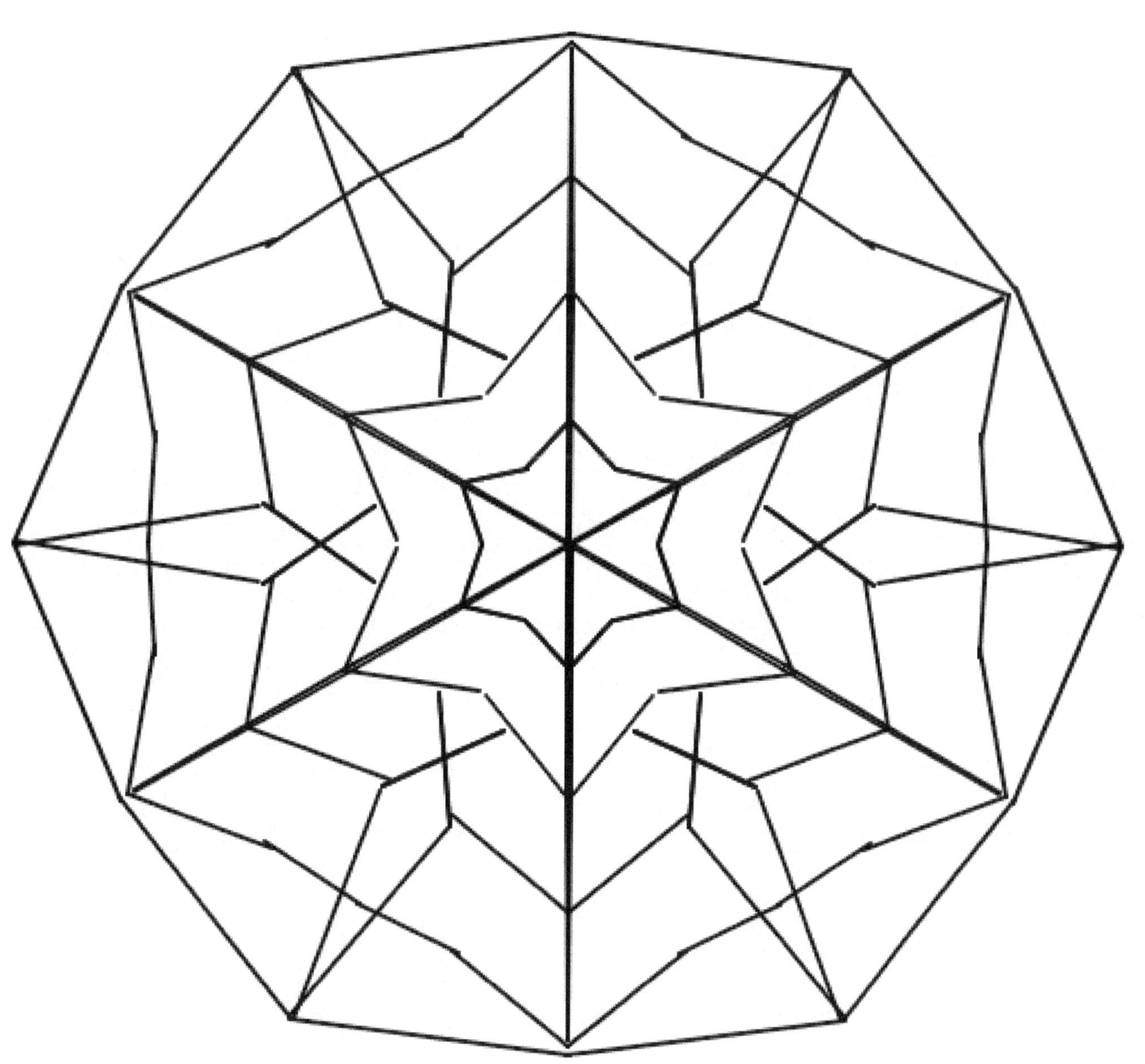

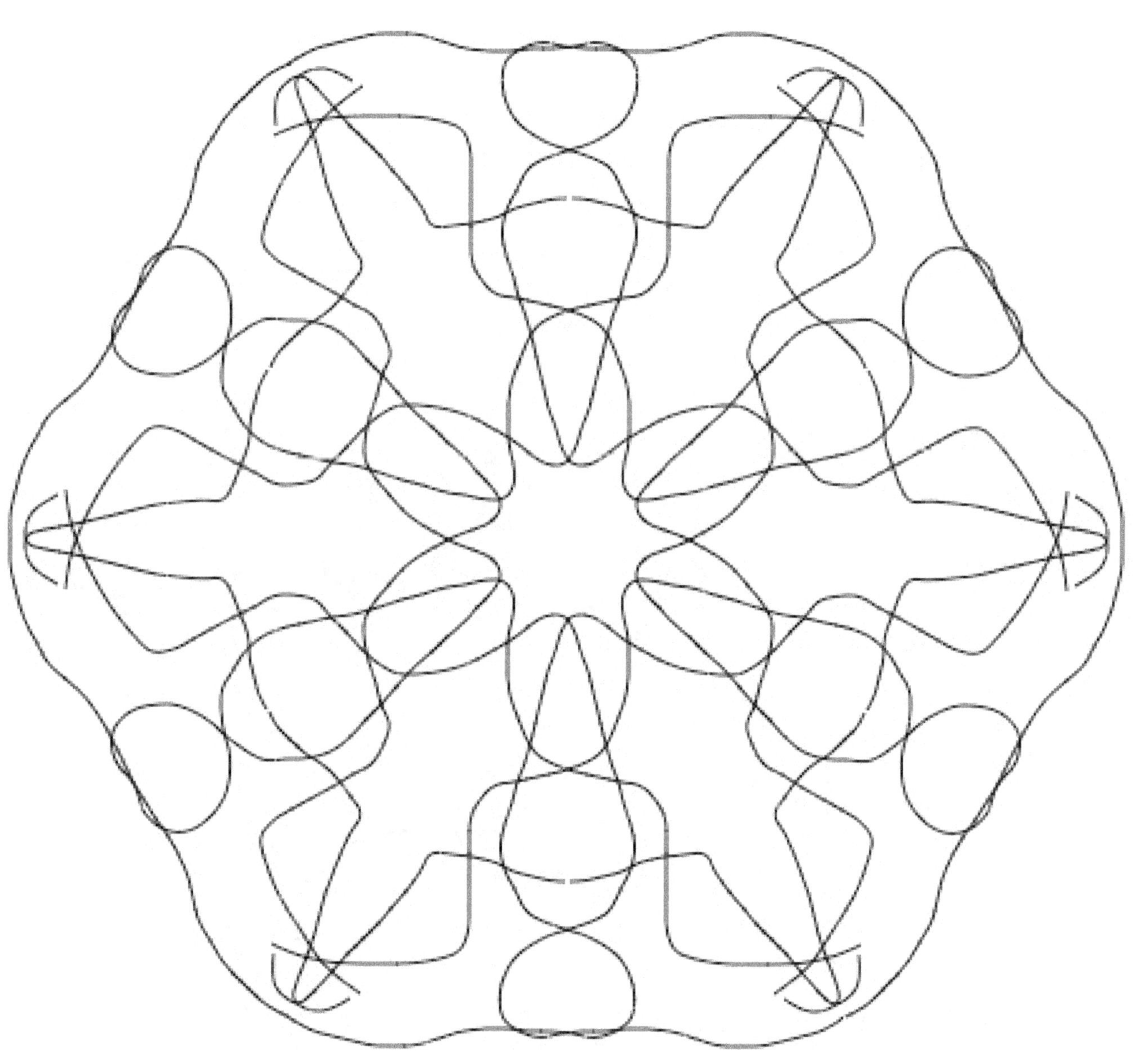

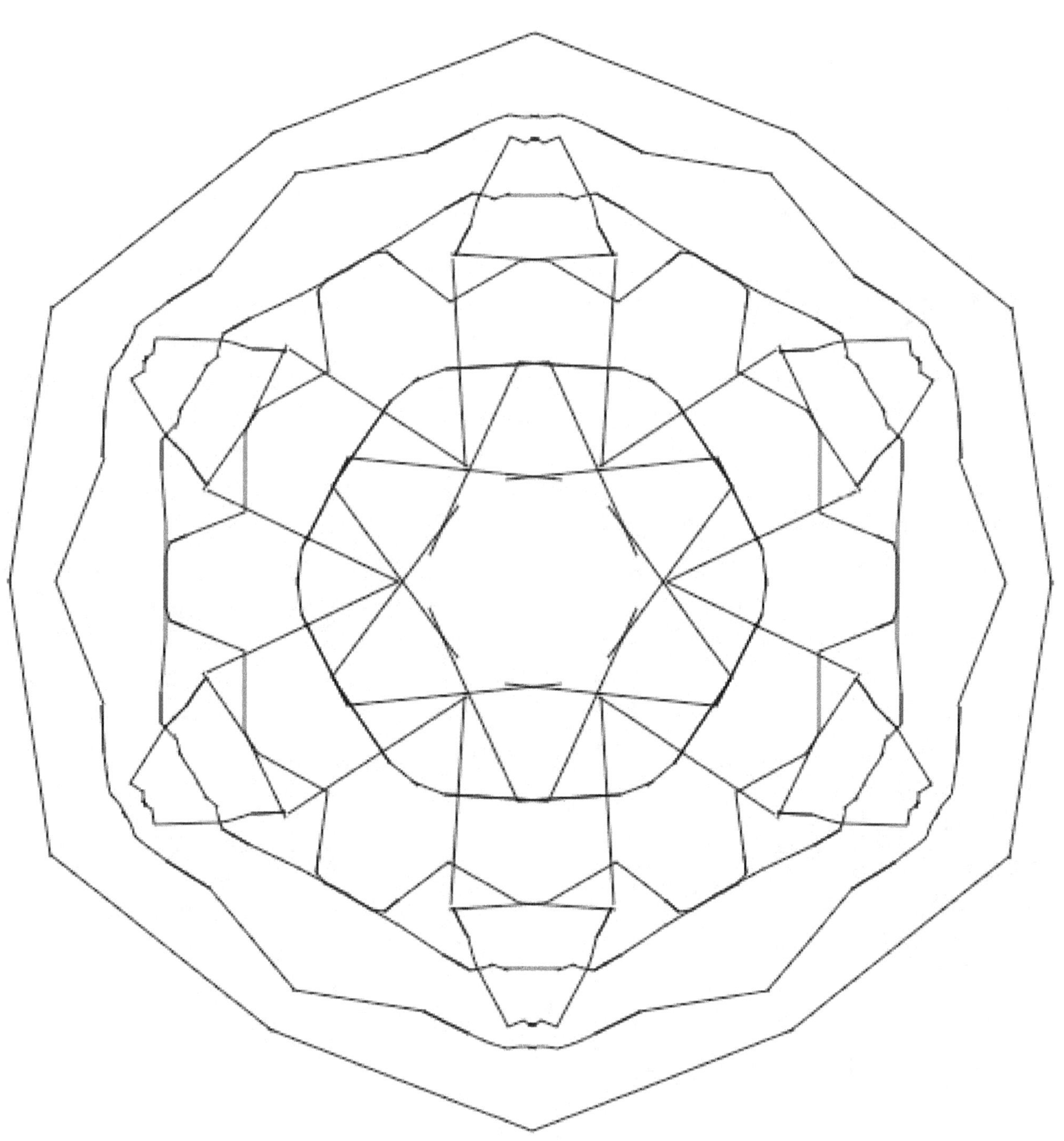

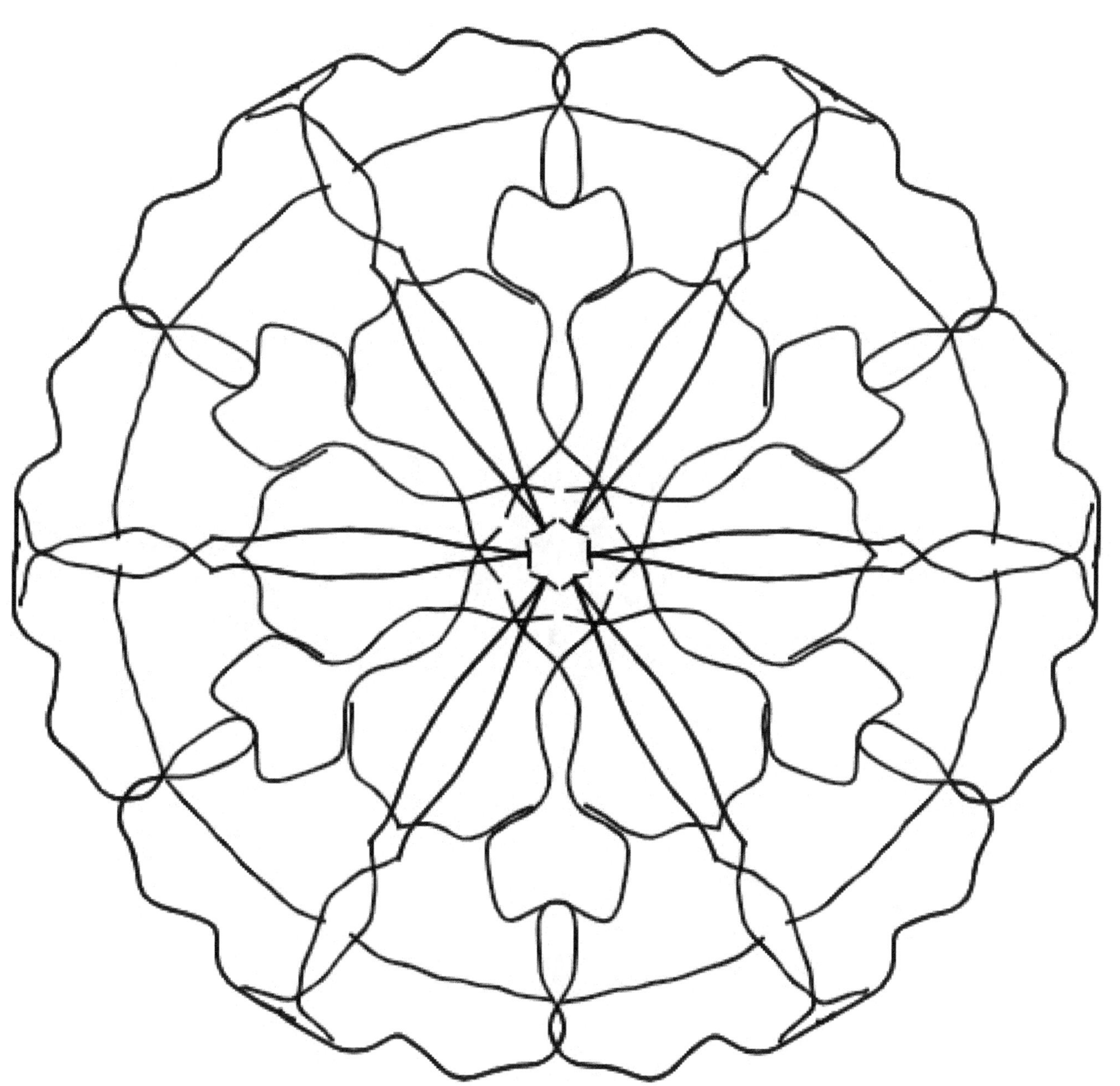

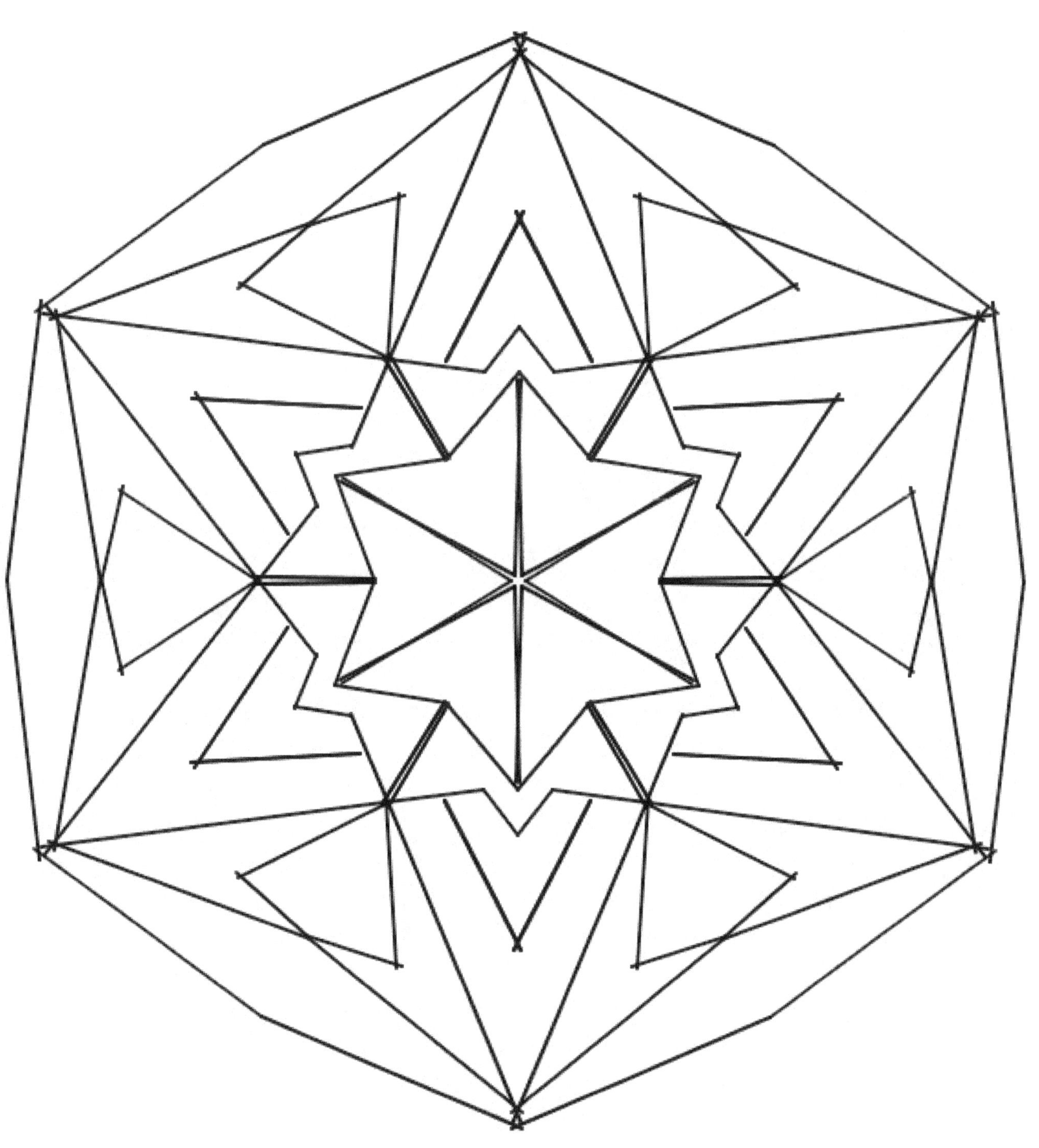

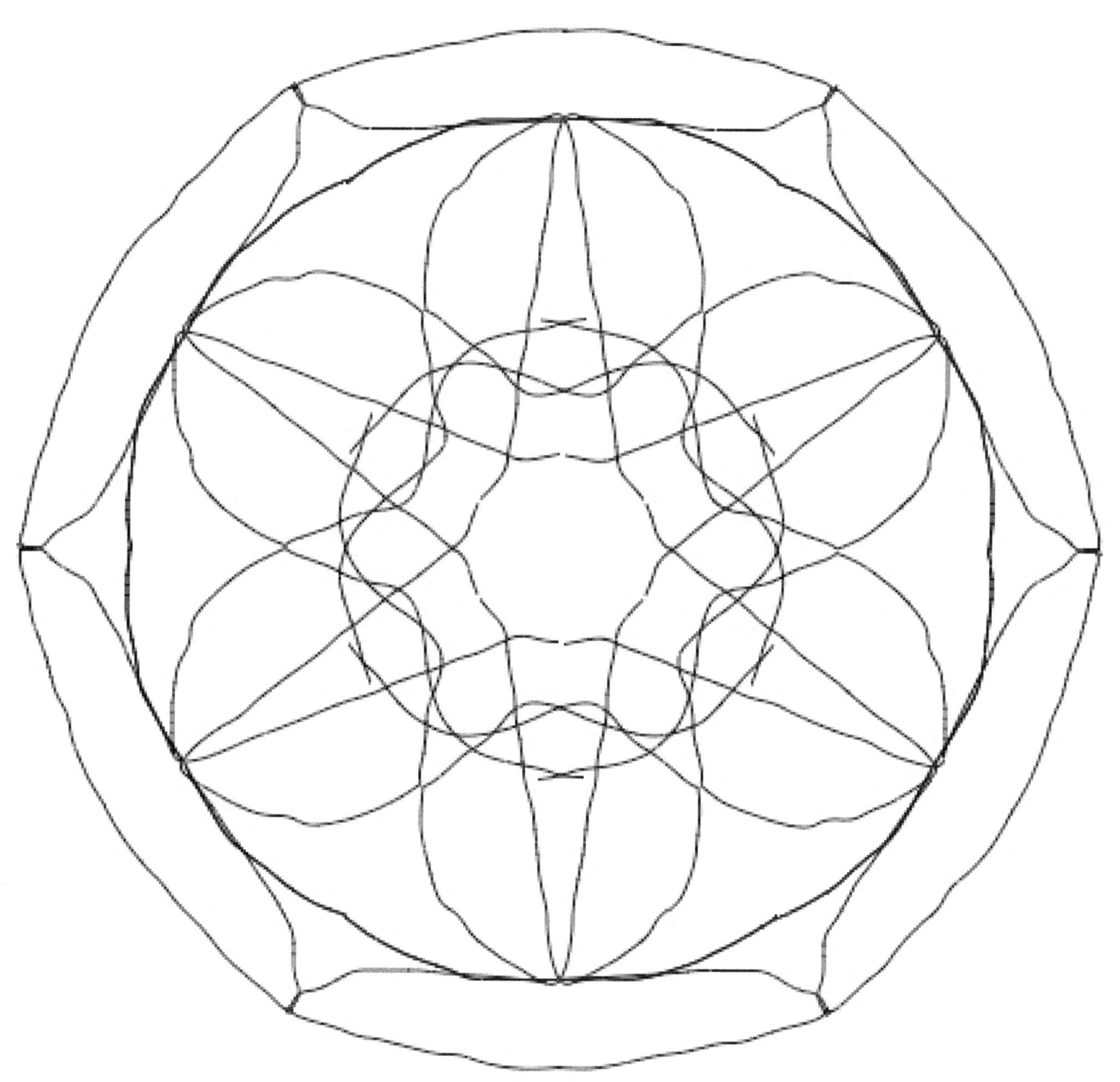

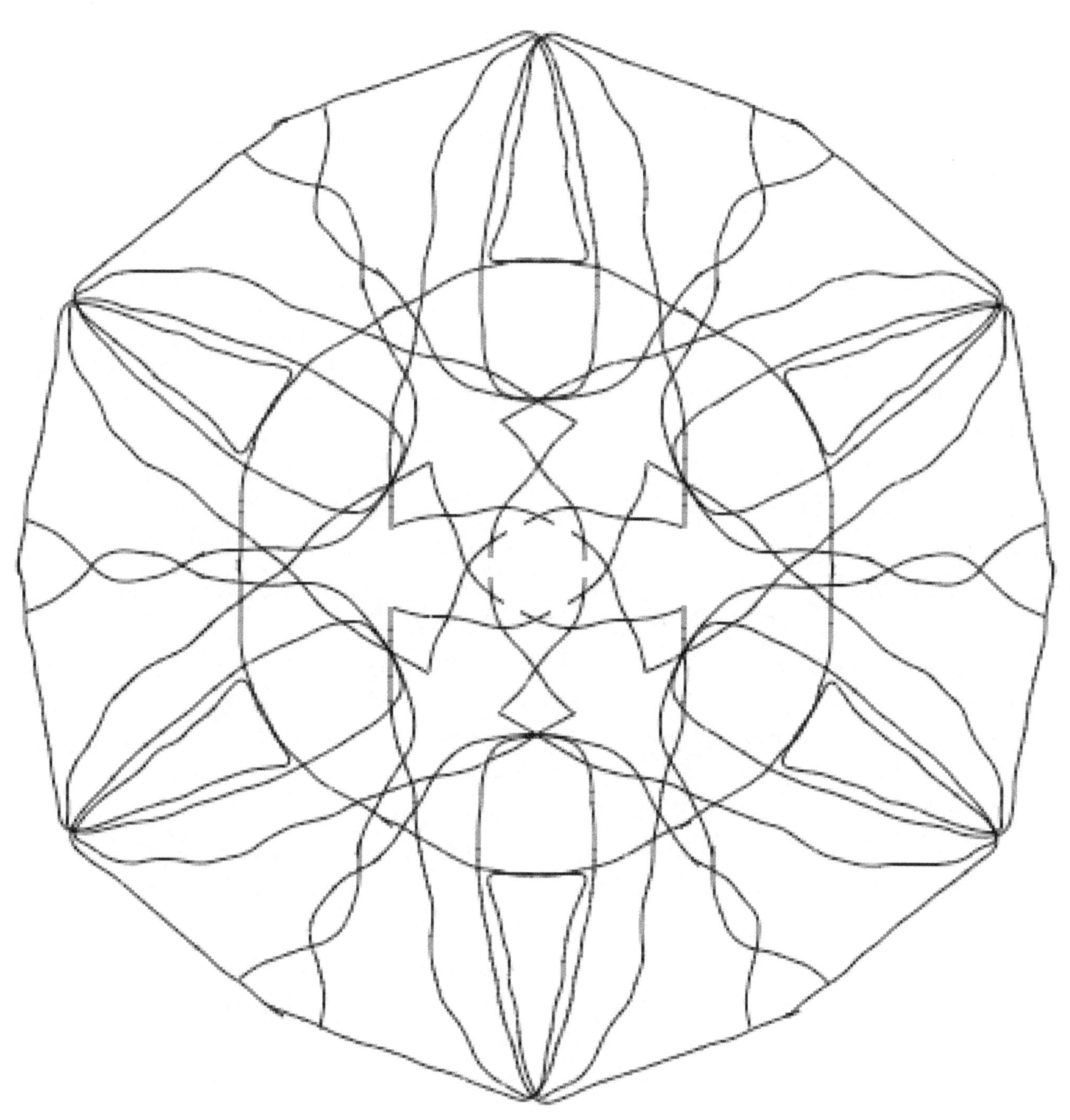

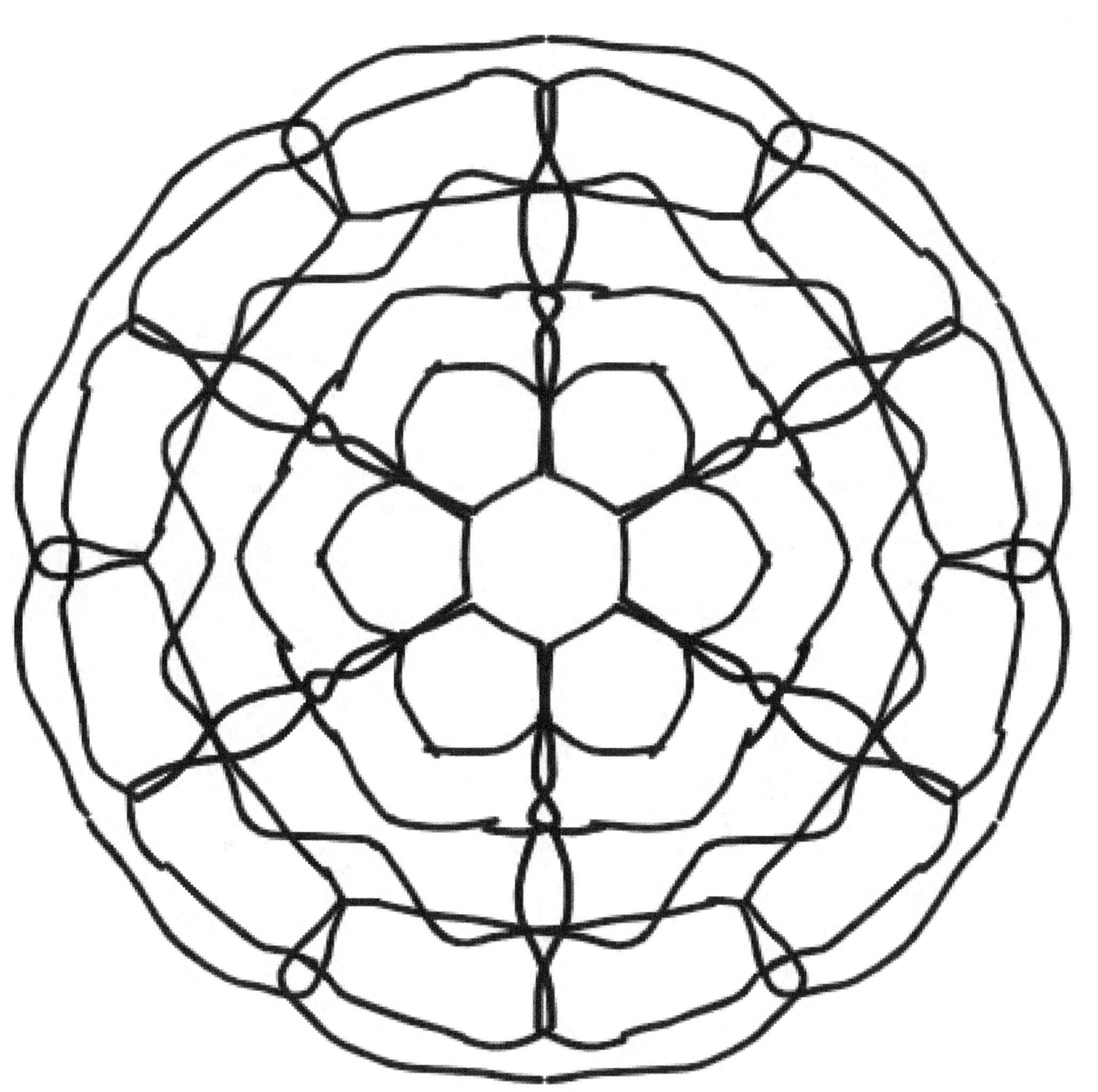

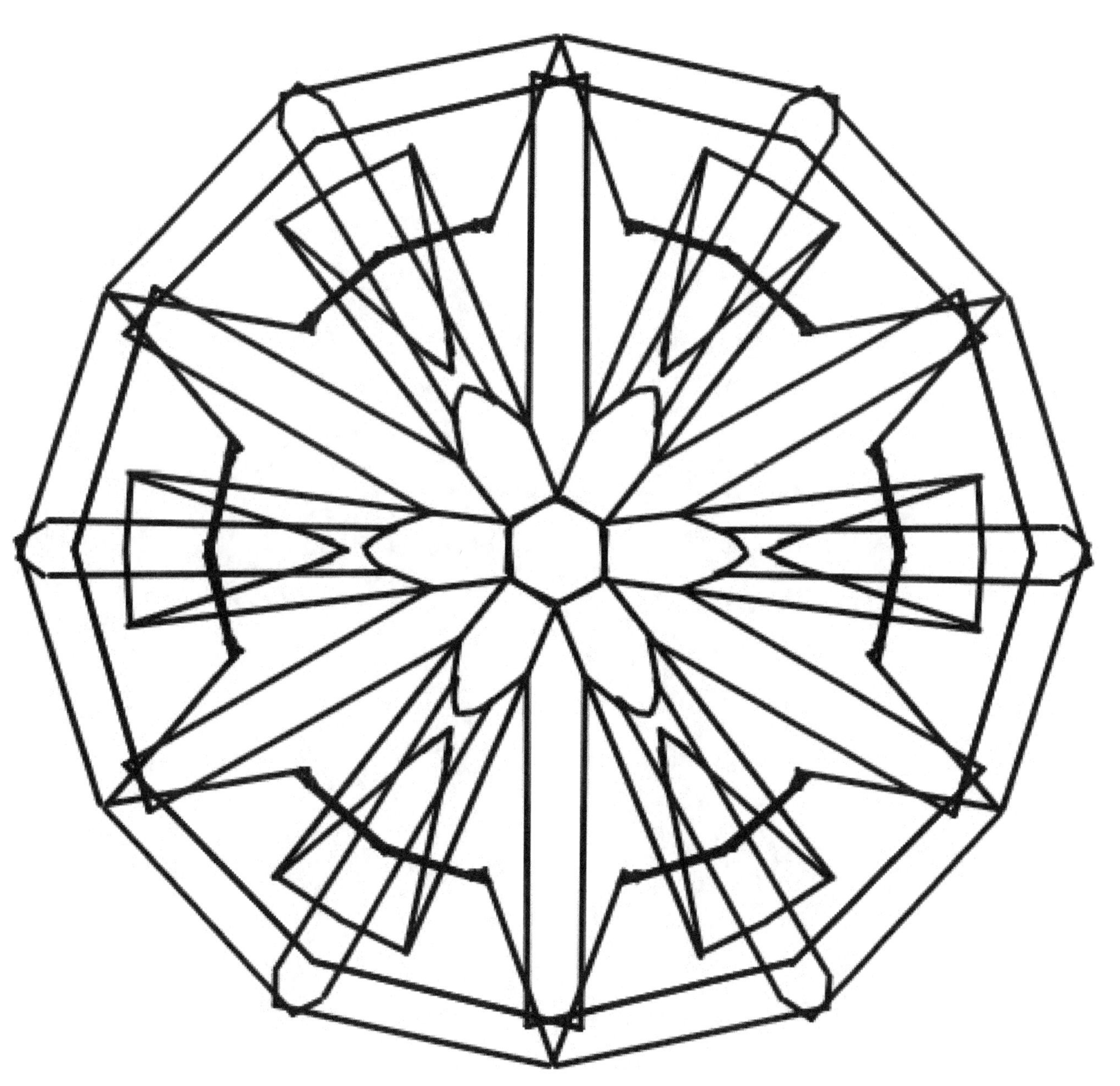

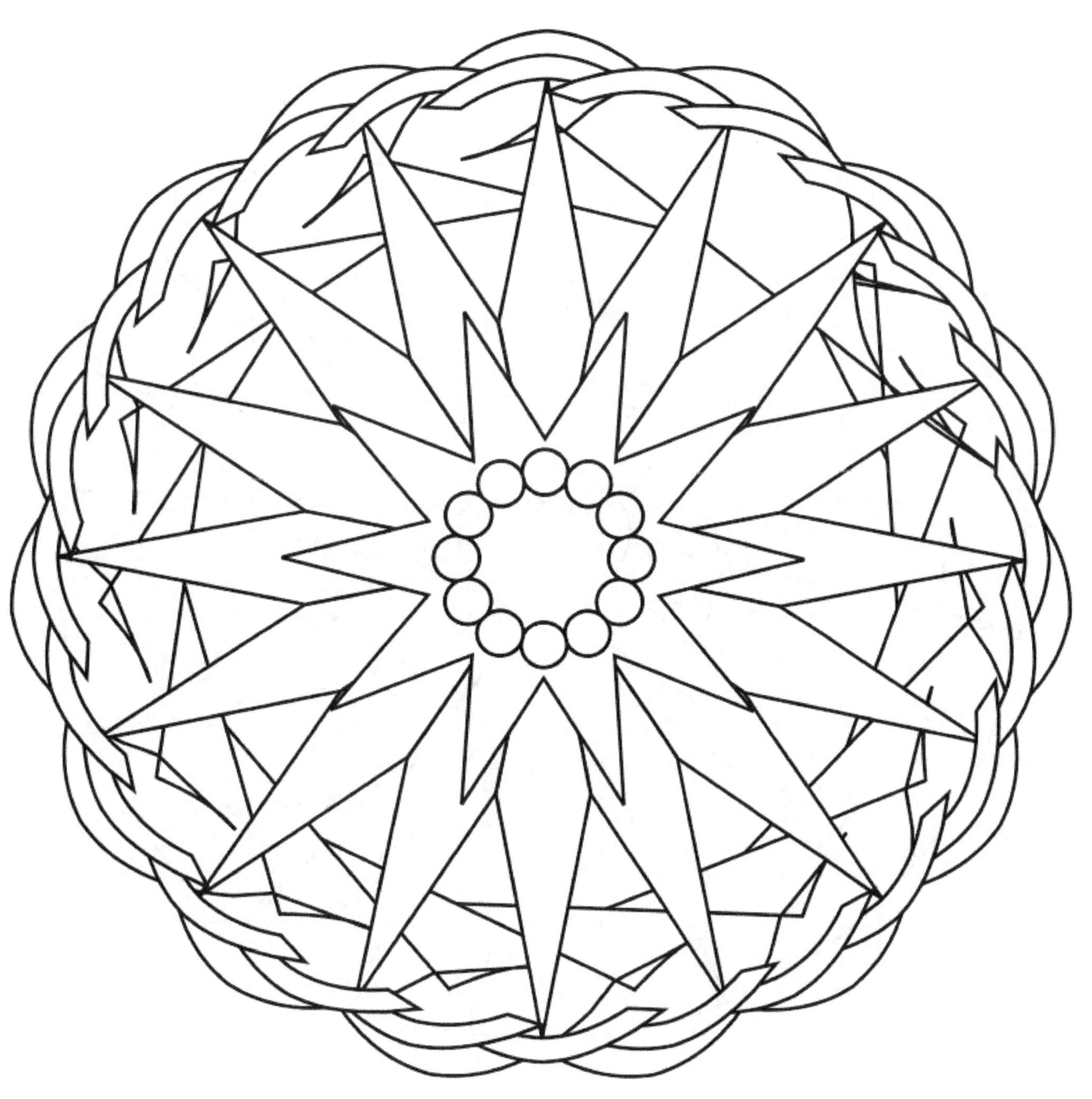

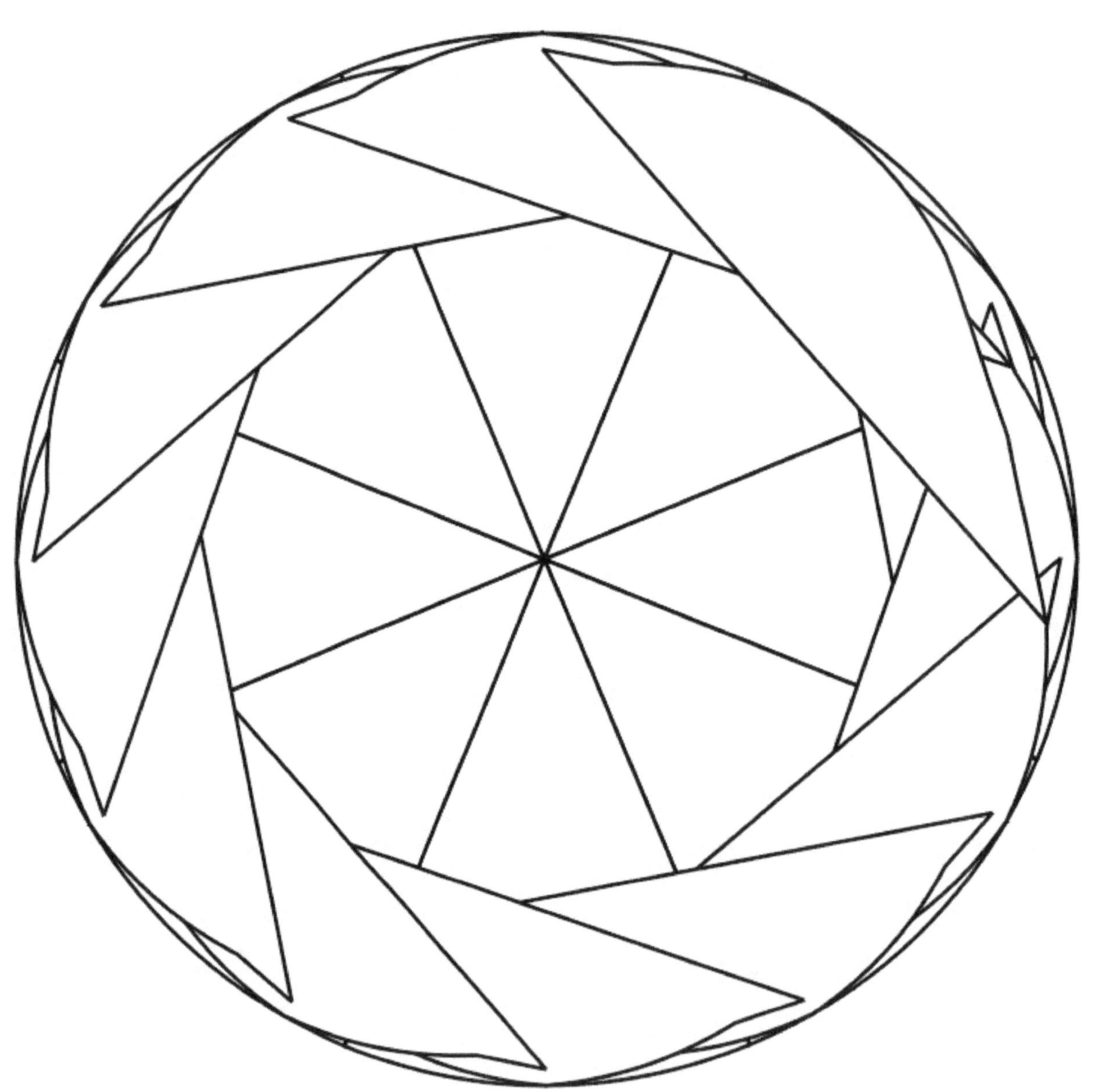